INVENTIONS

BIG IDEAS LOW INTERMEDIATE

JESSICA WILLIAMS

WAYZGOOSE PRESS

CONTENTS

INTRODUCTION

When you read an article or story, you have a conversation. The writer shares information, experiences, and ideas – but you, the reader, have your own ideas. When you read, you compare your experience and knowledge with the writer's ideas. Then you make decisions. Do you agree with the writer? Can you use the information to be healthier or more successful in your job, for example? Do you feel like the writer understands your life? Or do you learn about someone with a different point of view?

Because reading is a conversation, every reader experiences a text differently. When you read something interesting, you often want to talk about it. You want to share a similar experience, or you may want to argue. Maybe your friend understands the text in a different way. When you listen to your friend, you have a third set of ideas and experiences to compare to your own world view.

Big Ideas is designed to start interesting conversations between readers and writers, but also between readers and other readers. In this book, you'll learn about the history of many different inventions. Some of them, like lightbulbs, eyeglasses, and windshield wipers, are probably familiar to you. You probably see them or use them every day. Others may be new to you. Some, like pencils, are very simple; others, like bar codes, are very complicated. And some, like chewing gum, are a bit silly, but a lot of fun, while others, like moveable type and GPS, have changed the way we live. All of these inventions have interesting stories.

While you learn about interesting inventions, *Big Ideas* is also helping you develop language skills. Because our focus is on providing a positive reading experience, more than 90 percent of the words in this book are among the most common 2000 words in the English language. These are called "high-frequency words." High frequency words appear over and over again in speaking and writing.

You might think it will be easy to learn high frequency words, and it is true that many words are easy. Content words such as *tree, house, eat, drink*, and *blue* put a picture in your mind. They represent things you can see and name. They often have one meaning, and you can translate them easily.

However, many high frequency words change their meaning when they partner with other words in collocations. *Stay* is an example. When we say, *I stayed home yesterday*, then *stay* has a different meaning from *Let's try to stay awake all night* or *Stay away from the cookies. I'm saving them for the party*. This flexibility shows that *stay* does not just have one meaning. It adapts to the words around it.

Fortunately, there is a method to learn the different meanings of collocations: read a lot. When you read, you see words in different combinations, and you learn their meanings. This can happen naturally, but it will happen faster if you pay attention to words in groups. When you notice and highlight or copy word combinations, you can learn the different meanings.

You can also learn the grammar that goes with a vocabulary word. For example, you might see *educate* as a verb in *educate children*, *education* as a noun in *a college education,* and *educational* as an adjective in *an educational experience*. You will also notice that some verbs are usually followed by a preposition, such as *talk about* or *talk to*, while others are followed by a noun, as in *hear a bird*. These grammatical details are hard to hear in spoken English, but they are easy to see in a written text. Check the "Supplementary Materials" section for a link to tools for developing language awareness in this way.

While vocabulary has a strong relationship with grammar, grammar has a strong relationship with sentences. In order to give you a positive reading experience, we have used easy-to-read sentences. We use grammar from low and intermediate levels, and we reduce synonyms and idioms. Our goal is to keep the big ideas about inventions, but present them in simple language.

SUPPLEMENTARY MATERIALS

For *Big Ideas* downloadable learning tools for students and teachers, go to
https://wayzgoosepress.com/jessica-williams/

PART I

FOOD

The history of food and eating is, in many ways, simply human history. Everybody eats, right? But how often do you think about where foods come from, and why we eat the way we do?

Learning about the history of food can tell us about how people lived and worked in the past. It is also connected to the history of technology. Different ways to grow, save, store, and even pay for food change the way we eat, and they influence what we eat.

These three texts will take you back thousands of years and to all corners of our world.

1

CHEWING GUM

When you were in school, did your teachers tell you, "Don't chew gum in this class!"? They probably did. So why do so many people chew gum?

The answer goes back a long time. People started chewing gum more than a thousand years ago. Of course, back then, people did not chew the same kind of gum that we chew today. In the 14th century, the Aztec people of Mexico chewed the sap from a tree called *sapodilla*. They took the sap from the tree and let it dry until it was hard. Then they cut it into small pieces and chewed it. They called it *chicle*. The Aztecs chewed *chicle* when they were hungry or thirsty. After they chewed it for a few minutes, they did not feel as hungry or thirsty anymore.

Today some people still chew gum for the same reason. Perhaps they don't have time to eat, or they are on a diet and don't want to eat. The Aztecs also chewed *chicle* to make their breath smell better. Many people chew gum today – for the same reason.

Then the history of chewing gum took a strange turn. The sap from another tree is used for a completely different product: rubber. In the 19th and early 20th century, rubber was used everywhere – in cars, in homes, in hospitals. In the middle of the 19th century, Antonio López de Santa Anna got an idea for making money. Santa Anna was a general in the Mexican army, and later, the president of Mexico. But by 1854, he was no longer president, and he needed to make money. He knew that many people were making a lot of money in the rubber business. The sap from the *sapodilla* tree and the rubber tree are not very different. Santa Anna chewed *chicle* all the time, and so he thought, "There is so much *chicle* in Mexico. What if we could use *chicle* to make a kind of rubber?"

So, Santa Anna brought some *chicle* to an inventor in the United States named Thomas Adams. Adams worked with the *chicle* that Santa Anna brought. He tried to make a product like rubber. He tried to make toys, boots, and many other things, but he did not succeed. Santa Anna gave up on the idea, but Adams did not. He had a different idea. Why not use *chicle* in the same way as the Aztecs did – for chewing gum? So, he started a gum company. Adams' gum was almost a success, but it did have one problem: it had no taste. That soon changed when other companies began to add sugar, fruit, and mint to their chewing gum.

Perhaps the most famous gum company is the Wrigley Gum Company. However, it did not start as a gum company. When the company began, it sold soap. The company put a few pieces of gum in their boxes of soap as a kind of prize. Soon, the gum was more popular than the soap. So, William Wrigley, the head of the company, changed his business to chewing gum. He was not the first person to sell chewing gum, but he was the first person to advertise it all over the world. His advertisements and his gum were very successful. When he died in 1932, he was one of the richest men in the country.

Today, gum is still popular, but some teachers and parents still don't like it. What's wrong with gum? Some people think it looks ugly when people chew gum. Other people say gum is not healthy. Some people even say that if you eat gum, it stays in your stomach for seven years! (Not true!) Gum with a lot of sugar is not very healthy. That's true. However, some scientific studies show that gum without sugar is good. First of all, it can help clean your teeth. Second, it helps people feel more awake, and think more quickly and clearly. So, maybe your teachers were wrong. Maybe everyone should chew gum in school!

Reflection

1. Do you chew gum? Why or why not? What are some other reasons people chew gum?
2. People are buying less gum today than in the past. Why do you think this is happening?

DUMPLINGS

Dumplings. Almost every culture has them: *jiaozi* in China, *mandu* in Korea, *pierogi* in Poland, *manti* in Turkey, *tamales* in Mexico, and *fufu* in western Africa. And there are many more. A recent book has a list with more than a hundred different kinds of dumplings.

So, what is a dumpling? It's hard to say exactly, because not everyone agrees on the definition. But here is a good place to start: A dumpling is made of dough. Dough is some kind of flour mixed with liquid. But there are many kinds of flour. Flour can be made from wheat, corn, rice, or other grains. And there are different kinds of liquid, such as water, milk, or soup. There may also be other ingredients in the dough, such as salt or eggs, but the most important things in the dough are flour and liquid.

Those are the simplest dumplings. But not all dumplings are so simple. Most dumplings have something inside the dough, such as meat, vegetables, fruit, or cheese. Finally, how do you cook the dumplings? In general, you boil dumplings in hot water or soup, but you can also fry them in hot oil. There are so many different ways to enjoy dumplings!

The next question is why. Why do dumplings appear on tables

all over the world? Why are they so popular? There are probably several reasons.

First, they are an inexpensive way to fill a lot of stomachs. They are mostly made of flour, which is not very expensive. They are a good way to use little bits of food – a little piece of meat, a few vegetables – left from another meal. Just cut up the leftover food, put it inside some dough, and cook the dumplings. Now you have a delicious snack that everyone loves. Some families cannot buy a lot of meat, cheese, or even vegetables because they are too expensive. Dumplings can make a little bit of these foods go a long way. Finally, dumplings are easy to carry because they come in their own little package.

Another question that people often ask about dumplings is: Where did they come from? Did one person invent them? Did they start in one place and then move to other places? Or, did they appear in lots of different places independently? In other words, did lots of people in different places think, *Dumplings! What a great idea!* The answer is that both are probably correct.

The history of dumplings goes back a very long way. There were recipes for dumplings in Rome 2000 years ago. Dumplings in China also go back almost 2000. In China, there is a story about the first dumplings. A man named Zhang Zhongjing made dumpling soup as a kind of medicine. That's the kind of medicine that everyone likes!

Dumpling changed as people moved around. People took them along when they traveled, so other people tried them and liked them. Then those people made them with the kinds of food that they liked. People made the dough from whatever food they had. In Mexico, they used corn; in Europe they used wheat and potatoes; in Japan, they often used rice.

In China, many people believe that dumplings bring good luck. People eat dumplings during the New Year holiday to bring them money and luck in the coming year. Maybe they are right! Dumplings brought one Chinese businessman a lot of money. In

1992, Chen Zemin started a company that makes frozen dumplings and other frozen foods. Twenty years later, his company had seven factories. The biggest factory makes 400 tons (363,000 kg) of dumplings every day! Mr. Chen is a very rich man. Sometimes people call him the "dumpling billionaire."

Dumplings started as a simple food. Every culture had their own kind, but dumplings have changed as they traveled around the world. Some of the newest dumplings may surprise you. Today, you can find Japanese *gyoza* filled with American cream cheese... and *momos,* from Nepal, filled with chocolate!

Reflection

1. What kind of dumplings do people in your country eat? Describe them. Do you like them?
2. Can you think of other types of food that are popular all over the world?

3
___

FROZEN FOOD

Look in any supermarket. There are rows of freezers full of frozen food. You can buy strawberries in the middle of winter. You can find fish from the other side of the world. For thousands of years, humans have looked for ways to keep food fresh and safe. They added salt to meat. They dried fish. Later, they put vegetables in cans. This food is safe to eat, but it doesn't taste like fresh food. In the late 19th century, some people tried to freeze food, but the results were not very good. When it was cooked, the frozen food became very soft, it had no color, and it tasted terrible. And some of it was not very safe. No one wanted to buy frozen food.

All of that changed in the 1920s when a man named Clarence Birdseye started to think about frozen food. He was working in northern Canada, where the weather is very, very cold in winter. The native Inuit people there ate a lot of fish. In winter, they cut a hole in the ice to go fishing. When they took the fish out of the water, the fish froze immediately in the cold air. They kept the frozen fish for weeks. When they cooked the fish later, it tasted fresh and delicious. Birdseye was surprised and curious. Why was this frozen fish so good? And why was the frozen fish he had eaten before so bad? What was the difference?

He cut up small pieces of both kinds of frozen fish. He looked at them under a microscope. They looked very different. When food freezes, the water inside them turns into ice. Ice is made of crystals. In the delicious fish, these crystals were very small. In the old, soft fish, the crystals were much bigger. Birdseye finally understood. When you freeze food very quickly at a very low temperature, the ice crystals are small. If you freeze food slowly and the temperature is only one or two degrees below 32°F (0°C), the crystals are large. Large crystals make food soft. Birdseye knew he had a great idea for a business – the frozen food business.

Birdseye went home and started to work on his idea. He invented a machine that could freeze food very quickly and at a low temperature. He started his own frozen food company in 1924. He started with fish. In 1927, he froze 1.6 million pounds (726,000 kg) of fish. But there were other problems. How could he move his frozen food from one place to another? Where could he sell his frozen food? Most stores did not have freezers. And who would buy his frozen food? Most homes did not have freezers either. Birdseye had to wait for all of these things. He sold his company to a bigger company. In 1930, the bigger company decided to give freezers to ten stores, and things began to change.

Perhaps the biggest problem for frozen food sales was the memory of that old frozen food. Many people had tried frozen food before, and they did not like it. They also thought it wasn't safe to eat. It took a long time to convince them to buy this new kind of frozen food. But when they tried it, most of them liked it. It looked good and tasted good – almost as good as fresh food. It was also very convenient and saved a lot of time. For example, the frozen vegetables were already clean and cut into small pieces. In a few minutes, they were ready to eat. More families bought freezers for their homes.

Slowly, frozen food became more popular. People could eat

fruit and vegetable all year round. They could have a healthier diet. They could also try new foods – shrimp from Thailand, mangoes from the Philippines. Frozen food made the world a little smaller. Today, frozen food is a 240-billion-dollar business, and it is still growing. With frozen food and a microwave oven, some people never cook at all!

Reflection

1. Do you ever eat frozen food? Do you think restaurants ever serve frozen food? Should they?
2. Do you think it is good to be able to eat 'shrimp from Thailand' and 'strawberries in winter'? Why or why not?

PART II

HEALTH AND WELLNESS

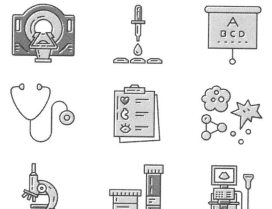

Three thousand years ago, most people died before they reached the age of 30. That age moved up a little over the centuries, but not much. In 1900, most people died before the age of 40.

However, in the last hundred years, all of that has changed, and the average age in many countries is closer to 70. The main reason for this change is that we are all much healthier because of improvements to the way we live and how we take care of ourselves.

In these three texts, you will learn about some of those improvements. Some are major, some are minor – but they're all important.

4

EYEGLASSES

Sixty percent of all people in the world need eyeglasses to help them see better. Today, most of those people need glasses to see far away. However, the first glasses were to help people see things that were close to them, usually books.

How did anyone get the idea to look through a piece of glass in order to see better? No one is sure, but the first "glasses" weren't made of glass at all. They were probably clear stones. People just held the stones and looked through them. The first person to notice that glass could change the path of light was a scientist named Alhazen (Ibn al-Haytham in Arabic) in Egypt in the eleventh century. He also noticed that glass could make things look larger. He wrote about his ideas in a famous book. It's likely that this information spread to other places, including China and Europe.

There are not a lot of written records from this time, so we are not sure when the first eyeglasses appeared. Most people believe that they appeared in Italy in the 13th century. Venice, Italy, was famous for making glass for other purposes. Early eyeglasses did not have the part that goes over your nose and around your ears. They were just pieces of glass in a special shape.

They were thicker in the middle and thinner at the ends. They looked like a kind of bean. The word for this kind of bean in Latin was *lentil*, so they got the name *lens*. That is the name we still use today for the glass part of eyeglasses.

In the beginning, people held these lenses over a page when they wanted to see better. At that time, there were not very many books because books were very, very expensive. They were expensive because someone had to copy each page with a pen and ink. Also, not very many people could read. So only a few people needed glasses.

That situation changed in the 15th century when a new invention appeared: the printing press. The printing press was a machine. It could print books quickly. Soon, there were more books, and more people learned to read. As a result, more people needed glasses. One reason we are not sure about the history is that these early makers of glasses wanted to keep their idea a secret. They knew they had a good idea, and they did not want other people to steal it.

Around this time, scientists began to make different kinds of lenses. One German scientist tested a lens with the opposite shape. It was thin in the middle and thick at the edges. He discovered that this kind of lens could help people who could not see far away. Other scientists began to find other uses for lenses; for example, to see things that were very, very small or things that were very far away. Of course, today, we call those inventions microscopes and telescopes.

Many more people are wearing glasses than in the past. Why? There are probably two main reasons. First, as we get older, it becomes more difficult to see things that are very close, like words on a page. Because people are living longer, there are more people who need glasses for reading. But why do so many more people need the other kind of glasses – the ones that help us see things that are far away? Scientists wanted to know why, so they studied the question.

One study suggests an explanation. The study looked at two groups of children. One group spent a lot of time outside in bright light. The other group spent a lot of time inside. The children who stayed inside were reading and working on their computers. More of them needed glasses to see far away when they were older. The scientists also noticed that in countries where education is very important, more people need this kind of glasses. For example, ninety percent of young people in China today need them. Only twenty percent needed glasses in 1960. Education is very important in China, and young people today study very hard. So, it you study a lot, you will probably need glasses!

Reflection

1. Do you wear glasses? If so, do you need them to see far away, or to read?
2. The number of people who need glasses to see far away is increasing. Do you think that number will continue to go up? Why or why not? Is there any way to stop it?

5

TOILETS

It has saved thousands of lives. It's a place you visit about 2000 times a year. But nobody wants to talk about it. In fact, for most people, it's just not polite to talk about it. What is it? It's your toilet. Toilets are very important to human health because they take away waste. If people have no toilets and live near human waste, they can get very sick. This can happen if the waste gets into their food or water. Many people have died for this reason. Today, people all over the world still get sick because they don't have a toilet.

Toilets are not a new invention. There were toilets in Rome in the first century and in Greece and Mesopotamia (where Iraq is today) before that. Their toilets were not so different from our toilets today. They used water to wash away waste. That is the most important part of a toilet. That is the part that can save lives.

But later, somehow, people forgot about the importance of toilets. They forgot about the best ways to deal with their waste. When people lived on farms, far away from each other, this was not a big problem. However, when lots of people started moving to cities, human waste did become a big problem. As cities grew larger, that problem got bigger and bigger. And the problem smelled really terrible. The population of the cities in Europe, such as London and Paris, grew very quickly in the 18ᵗʰ and early 19ᵗʰ century. Most people didn't have a toilet, and so they threw their waste in the street. A lot of that waste went into rivers. People washed in the river. They also drank water from the river. Yuck!

During this time, many people became sick, not just in Europe, but also in Asia, North Africa, and North America. There was a terrible disease called cholera. No one understood the cause of the disease then, but it killed tens of thousands of people. Today we know the cause of cholera was human waste in the drinking water. The best way to stop this disease is to separate people from their waste. For that, you need toilets. But toilets alone are not enough. The toilets also need a way to carry the waste to a safe place far away.

In the 19ᵗʰ century, these growing cities did not have either of these things – no toilets, and no system for removing human waste. Toilets were expensive. But what about a system to carry waste away from homes? That is *very* expensive. Who can pay for this system? Not one person or one family. You need a city or a country to pay for that. For a long time, cities did not want to pay. But more and more people died, and the smell got worse and worse. Also, scientists were learning more about the connection between human waste and human health. Finally, cities such as London, Paris, New York, and Chicago began to build systems to remove human waste.

Still, many people did not have toilets in their homes. Some people in London saw a toilet for the first time at the World's Fair in 1851. People could pay one cent to use the toilet at the fair. It was very popular. Almost a million people visited these toilets. Slowly, more and more homes in big cities got toilets. These cities became healthier places to live.

However, around the world, there are still four and a half

billion people who do not have a toilet. Many of them get sick with diseases like cholera. Some of them die. The United Nations is working hard to bring them clean water and toilets. The UN started National Toilet Day (November 19th) to remind everyone of this problem.

In the future, toilets will do more than carry away waste. Scientists are working on new kinds of toilets. They will be able to tell you about your health. Just think! Today you go to a doctor for information about your health. Perhaps in twenty years, you will just use your toilet. That's just one more step in the history of the toilet − saving lives and keeping us healthy!

Reflection

1. More people have a mobile phone than a toilet. Why do you think this is?
2. What do you think toilets will do for us in the future?

6

TOOTHBRUSHES AND TOOTHPASTE

It's not clear exactly when the first toothbrush and toothpaste appeared. Perhaps it was as early as 3000 BCE. It is clear, though, that clean teeth and fresh breath have been important for a long time. Well, actually that's true in some part of the world, but not everywhere. It may surprise you that most people in the United States didn't brush their teeth regularly (twice a day) until after World War II!

Toothbrushes started as simple sticks. People used them more two thousand years ago in Rome, China, and India. At about the same time, people in the Islamic world were using a stick called a *miswak* to clean their teeth several times a day. They used it when they woke up, after meals, and before prayers. Sticks work pretty well, but brushes work better. Brushes appeared a little later. The first toothbrushes were made from animal bones for the handle and animal hair for the brush. You can see toothbrushes like these in a museum in China. There were made in the eighth century BCE.

The idea of clean teeth took much longer to reach Europe. An Englishman named William Addis was probably the first person to sell toothbrushes in Europe. He was in prison because he hit someone during a fight. While he was there, his teeth (as well as the rest of his body) got very dirty. His breath smelled terrible. He also got bored because there was nothing to do. One day, he was looking at a broom. It gave him an idea for a way to clean his teeth. He found an old bone (on the floor!) for the handle. A person who worked in the jail helped him find some animal hair for the brush. It worked pretty well. So, when Addis got out of prison, he started a toothbrush business.

Addis sold a lot of toothbrushes, but they cost too much for ordinary people. The materials – animal bone and hair – were expensive. Starting in the 20th century, toothbrushes had plastic handles and nylon brushes. These materials were cheaper, so more people were able to buy them. During World War II, the U.S. soldiers got toothbrushes. They started brushing their teeth every day. They brought their brushing habit home after the war ended. The new habit spread, and more and more people started using toothbrushes.

Advertising also helped make toothbrushes popular. However, most of the advertisements were not for toothbrushes. They were for toothpaste. Toothpaste, too, has a long history. It goes back almost 5000 years. Egypt, Rome, Greece, and China all had some type of toothpaste. In 2003, someone found an old recipe for toothpaste from fourth-century Egypt. The recipe included salt, pepper, dried flowers, and small pieces of shells from nuts. A dentist read about this news and decided to try the recipe. He said it cleaned his teeth very well, but it also made his mouth bleed. He did not recommend it! He explained that most of these old toothpaste recipes are not very good for your teeth. Some of the ingredients are rough, almost like sand. Every time you brush with this kind of toothpaste, it removes a little bit of your teeth. If you brush like this for every day, your teeth will begin to break and fall apart.

Today, many toothbrushes are electric or use batteries. Today's toothpaste is gentle and does not hurt your teeth. It keeps them healthy and white. But these changes are small. They are really not so very different from what people used in the 18th century, or even earlier.

Toothbrushes and toothpaste are an ordinary part of our lives, so we don't think about them very much, but they are important. Doctors say that our mouths are the windows to our bodies. An unhealthy mouth often means an unhealthy body. Perhaps people understood that many years ago when they began to clean their teeth with sticks. People today continue to believe this. In 2003, a survey asked a question: Which invention would be the most difficult for you to live without? What was the number one choice? The toothbrush.

Reflection

1. What else do you use to stay clean? How old do you think those inventions are?
2. What invention do you think it would be the most difficult for you to live without?

PART III

SCHOOL AND OFFICE

Most of us spend about a third of lives at work. When we are young, we spend that time at school.

The place where we work and the tools we use make a big difference in how well we do our jobs and how much we enjoy them. We often take these tools for granted, but they have a significant impact on our daily lives.

In these three texts, you will learn about history of the places where we spend so much time and the tools we use there.

7

PENCILS

What is one of the most common items in the classroom, even in a time of computer technology? The pencil.

A thousand years ago, pens and ink were the most common writing tools. People also used pieces of burned wood and sticks made of lead and other kinds of metal. These were the first pencils, but they were not easy to use, because the metal inside was quite hard.

In 1564, in Cumbria, England, a storm pulled a tree out of the ground. Deep in the ground under the tree there was a large amount of a soft gray material. People thought it was a kind of metal. They called it lead. But it was not lead; it was not even a metal. It was a material called *graphite*. And it was perfect for writing. Farmers used pieces of graphite to make marks on their sheep. These graphite pieces worked even better on paper. They made a smooth mark as thin as a human hair. Today we know this material is graphite, but we continue to call the material inside a pencil "the lead."

Graphite was very useful for writing, but it did have one problem. Because it was soft, it made the writer's fingers dirty. So, people began to cover the graphite with a piece of string or cloth, and later with pieces of wood. In the 18th century, several pencil factories opened in Europe, and later, in the United States. The outside of the pencils was painted in order to hide the low quality of the wood. Yellow was the most common color. In fact, it is still the most popular color for pencils today.

The factories made some pencils leads of pure graphite, but pure graphite is very soft. So, the factories began to mix the graphite with clay. In this way, they were able to make some pencils with very soft lead and some with harder lead. A soft lead makes a dark mark, and a hard lead makes a light mark. The factories gave numbers to different levels of hardness. The most popular is number 2. One number 2 pencil can write 45,00 words or draw a line that is 730 miles (1175 km) long. Even today, when some people take tests such as the TOEFL, the IELTS, or the GRE, they use a number 2 pencil. The mark of a number 2 pencil is the easiest for a computer to read. Of course, now many people take these kinds of tests on a computer, but others still use paper and pencil.

One reason people like pencils better than pens is that if you make a mistake, you can erase it. But in the beginning, pencils did not have erasers. Instead, people used pieces of old bread to remove the marks they made. In the 19th century, people began to use rubber for many different things. A man named Hyman Lipman noticed that rubber could erase a pencil mark. He added a piece of rubber to the end of the pencil, and the pencil eraser was born. In England, an eraser is called "a rubber" because they were once made of rubber.

Some people still prefer to write with a pencil. Famous authors, including Ernest Hemingway and John Steinbeck, often used a pencil. Steinbeck sometimes used sixty pencils in one day! Although most people now use computers to write, pencil sales are still strong. Today, factories all over the world make about fifteen billion pencils a year. About half of all pencils come from

China. If you put all of those fifteen billion pencils end to end, they would go around the world 62 times!

Reflection

1. What is your favorite writing tool? Why do you prefer it?
2. Why do you think pencil sales remain strong even when so many people use computers and other technology?

8

THE PRINTING PRESS

Ask ten people what they think is the important invention in history, and many of them will say the printing press. They might even say that modern world started with the printing press. They might give the date of 1440 and the name of the inventor − Johannes Guttenberg. Are those the facts? What is the story behind the printing press?

The printing press actually introduced four new things at the same time: better ink, better paper, moveable type, and a machine that brought all of these together. The two most important ones were paper and moveable type.

Let's start with paper. Before the printing press, the pages of most books were made of animal skin. Preparing the skin took a long time, and it was very expensive. In Europe, the most popular book was the Bible. Just one Bible used the skin of 300 sheep! Miles away from Europe, the Chinese learned how to make paper from pieces of old cloth. This paper was much cheaper and much better quality than paper made from animal skin. The Chinese tried to keep their recipe for paper a secret, but it was too valuable. Everyone wanted to know how to make paper. During a battle, Arab soldiers took some Chinese paper makers as prisoners. Soon the Arabs knew how to make paper. Soon after that, knowledge of this new kind of paper arrived in Europe.

Moveable type was the most important part of the printing press. To understand the importance of moveable type, you need to understand the old way of making books. People in Europe copied books by hand, with a pen and ink. But in China, they found a better way. A man named Bi Sheng made blocks from clay. On each block, he made a letter. He put ink on the blocks and then pressed the blocks on paper. This was much faster than copying by hand. However, this did not become popular in China for one main reason. Chinese does not have letters like English. Instead, it has thousands of *characters*. Each character is a different word. So Bi Sheng had to make thousands of different clay blocks. It was not very efficient, so printing this way did not become popular in China.

However, in Europe, the situation was very different. Most of the languages in Europe use an alphabet, and those alphabets have fewer than 30 letters. As a result, printers don't need very many different blocks. They can use the same blocks over and over. Johannes Guttenberg was a metal worker, so he decided to make the blocks in metal. They were strong and lasted a long time.

Guttenberg also used a new kind of ink. Before this time, the ink in books was a kind of paint. It was made from eggs. The new paint – and the new ink – was made from oil. It was much easier to use. Guttenberg also used the new paper, the kind made from cloth. Then he found an old machine that was used for making wine. It pressed all of the juice from grapes. He changed the machine a little bit, so it could press the ink onto paper. He put the blocks in a line, 42 lines on a page. He put some ink onto the blocks and put the paper on top. Then he pressed the blocks and paper in his machine. The result? A printed page.

Guttenberg could print 300 pages a day. His most famous book was the Bible, printed in 1455. He printed about 180 copies.

His Bible had 1286 pages and used 2500 blocks per page. It weighed 14 pounds (6.3 kg). How long would it take to make those 180 copies the old way – by hand? About 200 years!

Guttenberg's books were very popular. Soon, he was printing other kinds of books, not just Bibles. He printed poems, stories, and grammar books. More and more people began to read. Guttenberg tried unsuccessfully to keep his new technology a secret. Other people tried to make similar machines, and many of them succeeded. By the year 1500, there were more than 2500 printing presses in Europe and more than 5 million books.

The printing press caused an information revolution. It could produce a lot of information quickly and accurately. Suddenly, people could share important ideas and information. Scientists could read other scientists' work. There was a great increase in works of literature, science, and philosophy. Ordinary people could learn about many different things. They could read the Bible by themselves. This meant that the church could not control people as easily as in the past. New ideas and knowledge spread quickly all over Europe and to other parts of the world. The printing press changed the world forever.

Reflection

1. What other changes do you think occurred as a result of the printing press?
2. Have there been inventions since the printing press that are equally important? What are they? Why do you think they are of equal importance?

9

THE OPEN OFFICE

What do most big offices look like? What does your office look like? If it's like most other big offices, it has rows and rows of desks or tables. This design is called an "open office." Who thought of this as a way to organize an office? Have offices always been like this? And is it a good idea for business?

The open office has been around for at least a hundred years, but it started for a reason that may surprise you. Early open offices were a response to older, more traditional office plans. In traditional offices, the top boss had the office in the corner with a big window. Other managers had smaller offices with smaller windows. Secretaries had smaller offices with no windows, and so on. Every employee knew his or her place, based on the size and location of the office. The open office was an attempt to change this – to make offices more democratic. The idea was to make employees more equal by removing the walls between them.

The first the open offices were at big, successful companies. The best early open offices had lots of light and space between each desk. Then other, smaller companies copied the design. They made changes in the design to save money. The desks moved closer together. The rooms got darker and more crowded.

These open offices were noisy. It was difficult to have a private conversation, and it was almost impossible to concentrate. Although the goal of the open office was equality, the real effect was quite different. Employees began to feel like nameless parts of a big machine.

In general, employees, especially women, did not like the open office design. In the 1970s and 1980s, more and more women began to work in offices. For them, a quiet and private space was especially important. So, a new office design began to appear. In this design, the spaces for each employee were still small, but they had walls. However, the walls were short – only about five feet (1.5 m) high, and most spaces only had two or three walls, not four, and no door. The spaces were more private and less noisy. These small offices were called cubicles.

This plan lasted about 20 years, and then the open office began to come back. Why? Workers in the cubicles were not talking to one another. As the 21st century began, many new businesses were in computer and information technology. This new technology required teams of people to work together and share ideas. The offices of technology companies used a new kind of open office. The goal of the new open office design was to help people communicate easily and often. People could meet in shared spaces and discuss new products and projects. There was one more reason for the return to the open plan. This was a time when more and more communication became electronic. People were spending a lot of time answering email. Open office designers thought that people could save time by having a quick conversation, instead of answering email messages.

However, the new open office design has many of the same problems as the old open office design. Many employees don't like it. Studies have looked at how these offices work. It's still hard for employees to concentrate in open offices. It's also difficult for them to speak honestly when everyone near them can hear their conversations. With no door or wall, it's easy for other employees to interrupt them. For all of these reasons, employees don't get as much work done as they might in a private office. They are often less creative because they can't concentrate. These conditions also create a lot of stress. Many employees who work in open offices wonder: Does the open office design help people communicate, or does it just save the company money?

Despite all of these negative points, 70 percent of all offices still have some sort of open office design. This is starting to change, however, especially in big technology companies. Some of these companies now have offices with many different kinds of spaces. Each space is for a different purpose. Some spaces are quiet and private, for people who need to work alone. Other spaces encourage employees to work together. They are also comfortable spaces that look more like rooms in a home than an office. This kind of office is expensive, however. So, this change will probably not spread quickly, and many companies will probably keep their open office design.

Reflection

1. If you work in an open office, what do you like or dislike about it? Do you think it has met any of the goals described in the reading? If you don't work in an open office, do you think you would like it? Why or why not?
2. What do you think the offices of the future will look like? How will they be different from the open office?

PART IV

BUSINESS AND INDUSTRY

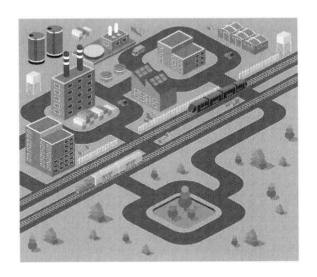

In English, there is an expression, "Money make the world go around." That may not be completely true, but business – making and spending money – is certainly a central part of modern life.

It is so central that sometimes we stop thinking about it. We stop asking questions, like "Where did that idea come from?" "Who first thought how to do that, and why?"

These three texts give you some answers to questions about business and industry that maybe you never even thought about!

10

BAR CODES

When I was young, I hated to go to the supermarket. The cashier checked each item to find the price. Then she entered the price into a machine. The machine added all the prices, and then my mother paid the bill. It took forever!

One day in June 1974, in a supermarket in Ohio, shopping entered the future. On that day, the cashier used a laser to "read" a very small label on a pack of chewing gum. That small label was the first UPC (Universal Product Code), which most of us call a "bar code." It is a series of black and white lines, and it appears on thousands of products, from peas to soap. Bar codes are now familiar to all of us. No one really thinks about them anymore. But in 1974, the bar code was big news.

I was not very patient with the long lines in the supermarket, but the store owners were even more unhappy than I was. It was difficult for them to manage all of the items in their stores. They were never sure how many of each product they sold. They didn't know when they needed to order more of something. They also had to pay cashiers to work in those long lines of unhappy customers. It was time for a change.

Engineers worked on this problem for a long time. One engineer invented an early bar code back the 1940s, but lasers at that time were too big and expensive, and store owners did not want to buy them. The bar code had to wait for laser technology to improve.

By the 1970s, laser technology was more advanced, so it was time to try the bar code again. The 1940s bar code was in the shape of a circle, but it was difficult to print the circle code accurately. Store owners wanted a better one. They asked 14 companies to design a new bar code. They wanted a bar code that was no bigger than 1.5 square inches (about 9 cm²). They also wanted a bar code that the cashier could read from 1.5 feet (about .5 m) away, and from any direction. This was not an easy job. In the end, an engineer from the IBM company offered the best solution.

That engineer, George Laurer, had two important ideas that made the bar code better. First, he made the label into a square. The square was easier to print accurately than a circle. Laurer's bar code has two kinds of information:

1. The name of the company that makes the product
2. The name of the product.

For example, (1) *Coca-Cola* is the company, and (2) a *one-liter bottle of Diet Coke* is the product. The bar code does not include the price. The supermarket decides on the price because different supermarkets might choose different prices. However, the product will always be a one-liter bottle of Diet Coke, made by the Coca Cola Company.

Second, Laurer made an important change in the laser that reads the bar code. The older lasers read codes with one thin, straight line of light. Laurer designed a laser to read barcodes with an X. The X shape made it easier to read all of the lines on the square bar code correctly. Some companies were afraid that the lasers would not be accurate. People at Birdseye, the frozen food company, thought that the ice on their boxes might cause problems. But frozen peas, even when their box was covered with ice, were not problem for the laser. The bar code worked perfectly. Today, five billion bar codes are scanned every day in stores all over the world.

With the bar code new technology, store owners got a lot of important information. They knew exactly how many of each product they had in the store. They knew how many they sold. They also had information about which products were popular with shoppers. Bar codes gave them a lot more control. With this control, bigger stores were now possible – really big stores, like IKEA and Walmart. It became difficult for small stores to compete with these large stores.

Today there are many different kinds of bar codes in different parts of the world and in different areas of business. Amazon has its own bar code system. Fedex has its own bar code system. The United States Post Office has its own bar code system. Look on the back of a book and you will see a bar code. Every year brings a new way to use them or improve them. It's hard to imagine a time before bar codes.

Reflection

1. How have bar codes affected jobs? Some kinds of jobs have disappeared, but there are also new jobs as a result of this technology. Think of some examples of each.
2. Can you think of any products for sale that do not have bar codes? Why don't they, do you think?

11

LIGHT BULBS

Thomas Edison invented the light bulb, right? Well, not exactly.
Edison wanted everyone to believe that he invented the light bulb
in 1879, but in fact, many different people were part of the invention. Edison did not do it alone. Different inventors, both in
Europe and the United States, were working on it in the 19th
century. Each of them helped with some part of the invention.
Edison bought, borrowed (some say, stole), and built on all of
these ideas. His light bulb, called an *incandescent* bulb, became
popular because it was cheap, reliable, and it lasted a long time.
None of the other inventors had a product like that.

Edison was also a good salesman. He was able to convince the
public that his light bulb was the safest and best light bulb. Many
people were worried that light bulbs were not safe. And, at first,
electricity and electric light bulbs did have a lot of problems.
Some people were hurt, and some were even killed by electricity.
So, Edison sent some of his workers to walk through the streets
of New York with light bulbs on their heads. The light bulbs were
turned on. Edison wanted to show everyone that his products
were safe.

Soon the public began to buy light bulbs — more and more

every year. They were so much cleaner and cheaper than older forms of light. With an electric bulb, a day's wages could buy 12,000 hours of light! Edison had a laboratory with dozens of scientists and engineers. They worked very hard to make their bulbs better and better all the time. Other companies tried to compete. They fought Edison in any way they could, but Edison almost always won.

Edison's light bulbs changed business and industry in very important ways. They changed the way all of us live. Perhaps the biggest change was in industry. With electric light bulbs, factories could stay open 24 hours a day. People worked all through the night. Factories could produce much more of everything and do it more quickly. More people made more money. They spent more money. The economy grew.

Light bulbs also changed home life in many ways. First, before the light bulb, many homes did not have electricity. But that began to change. When a house got electricity, the same electric wires that went to the lights became available for other products, such as washing machines and vacuum cleaners. All of these machines made housework easier, especially for women. Second, electric light allowed people to stay up later, after the sun set. With this extra time, they could read, study, and later, listen to the radio or watch TV. For the first time, the evening became a time for entertainment.

Soon there was more entertainment outside of the home as well. Before the electric light, city streets could be frightening places after dark. With light, an evening in the city became something quite different. Crime decreased. Night became a time to have fun. Restaurants, theaters, and clubs stayed open until early in the morning. The entertainment business was born.

Another important form of entertainment became more popular with electric light: sports. Before, sports were normally played during the day, when the sun was shining, and most games were played on weekdays. Because most people worked six days a week, they could not attend games. When sports teams began to play in the evening, suddenly the stadiums were full of people. Sports grew into a business that is worth millions of dollars today.

At the end of the 19th century and the beginning of the 20th century, thousands of people moved to the cities. Cities had jobs and entertainment. You might say that the electric light made our modern cities possible.

Of course, not everything that the light bulb brought was good. Some people believe they have made it more difficult for people to sleep. Edison only slept about three or four hours a night, so maybe he thought this was a good thing! Perhaps with all those hours of light, we work too hard. In addition, the bright lights create problems for some animals. Every year, more than 900 million birds die when they fly into the windows of buildings at night. They are confused by the electric lights inside the buildings.

Edison's company, General Electric, was very successful, and his light bulbs were used all over the world for more than 100 years. But incandescent bulbs are not very efficient. Only ten percent of their energy becomes light and the other 90 percent is wasted. Today, there are newer, more efficient light bulbs, but Edison's role in the history of the light bulb will remain.

Reflection

1. In one day, how much do you depend on electric light bulbs? What activities would be impossible without them?

2. Think of another important invention. What changes in society did it cause? Which are some positive, and which are negative?

12

LOGOS

They are everywhere and very familiar to all of us: the yellow **M** of McDonalds, the three red diamonds of Mitsubishi, the yellow and green flower of British Petroleum (BP). They are logos, and they help us to connect products to the companies that make them. Logos can be pictures, words, or phrases. Often the company's logo is just its name. It seems like an obvious idea. Have businesses always had logos?

A thousand years ago, people didn't travel far from their home, and so everyone knew everyone. They probably didn't need logos. But as both people and products moved across longer distances, the need to mark products and property increased. The first marks probably just showed the property owner. Starting in about the 11th century, the first business marks – perhaps the first logos – began to appear. Metalsmiths – that is, people who make metal products, such as swords or gold rings – put small marks on their products. Usually these were their names or initials.

Let's move ahead about 600 years. Most shops had a sign outside, with the name of the owner and the product or service: Simon's Tailor Shop, for example. Simon might also sew a small label with his name on the inside of the coats and suits that he made. If Simon was a good tailor, when people saw his label on a suit, they knew it was good quality.

But what if another tailor decided to sew a Simon label inside his coats? That's exactly what happened in England in the 17th century. That is when the government passed a new law to help people like Simon. The law said that the label – in other words, the logo – belonged to Simon. He owned it. For the first time, logos became property.

That was an important point in the history of logos. Business owners began to understand the power of logos, and more and more companies started using them.

So, how do companies pick a logo? Early logos were often names or pictures of the product, like Twining's Tea. Many companies still just use a name because the name is familiar; for example, SONY or IKEA. But soon some companies began to use pictures to create an image for their company. For example, the Peugeot car company's logo is a lion, to show that their cars are strong.

Today, life moves more quickly, and people don't have much time. Logos have changed to fit the modern world. Today, the best logos are simple, and easy to read and remember. People who look at a logo should be able to recognize it in just a few seconds. Just as importantly, they should not mistake it for any other logos. In addition, many companies today are international, so it impor-tant for people all over the world to recognize the logo. For all of these reasons, logos today are often simpler than logos of the past.

A simple logo may still be just a name, but it is also common today for companies leave out their names and only use the picture part of their logo. After the public becomes familiar with a logo that includes both a name and a picture, the name is no longer necessary. For example, the Starbucks logo used to include the name of the company. Today, it is just the picture of a mermaid. An early Pepsi logo included the word *Pepsi* inside a bottle cap. In other words, it showed both the company's name and a picture of the product. But that is not necessary anymore. Today's Pepsi logo is just a circle of red, white, and blue. Similarly, Facebook's logo started as the whole word, *Facebook*, and is now just an **f**. Even though these logos have no words, everyone recognizes them and their companies.

These logos are valuable. Companies pay a lot of money to create and protect them. Laws protect them against other companies that try to copy their logos. It's against the law for a company that sells a similar product to use a similar logo. If the companies sell very different things; however, it's usually not a problem. For example, the logos for Pepsi and Korean Airlines are very similar, but no one would confuse the two products. But if Pepsi started an airline, they would have a problem!

Logos are small, but they are powerful. They send a message about the company, and they help sell its products. Next time you see a logo, ask yourself, "What is the message? What effect does it have on me?"

Reflection

1. What is your favorite logo? What product or company does it represent? What is its message?
2. Why do you think some logos work better than others? Explain your answer with some examples.

PART V

TRANSPORTATION

Transportation means how people move from one place to another, and also how they carry and move goods – everything from clothing to tools to food.

The earliest form of transportation (other than our feet!) was animals, like horse and camels. After that, the history of transportation is a history of technology. New inventions changed the ways that people carried themselves and their things through their own cities and around the world.

Every century brought new improvements that moved people and things more quickly, safely, and comfortably. In these three texts, you will learn some of that history.

13
─────
GPS

Imagine you are driving in a city you don't know. You have an appointment in a building you have never seen. You check your smartphone or the system in the car, and it tells you the fastest way to get to your destination. It's simple and accurate. Now consider the same situation in your parents' time. There were no smartphones with apps to give them directions. If they owned a car, they stopped and looked at a map, or they asked someone on the street for help.

How did we get from then to now? The answer is GPS – the Global Positioning System – the system that can tell us the location of anything from the doctor's office to the closest Thai restaurant.

In the beginning, GPS was only for the government, only for the military. During the Cold War (1947-1991), the United States and the Soviet Union were searching for ways to get information about each other. Both countries sent satellites high above Earth to find that information. These satellites send out radio waves. In 1957, a U.S. scientist realized that these radio waves could give us important information about location of things on Earth. In the beginning, however, this was a secret project. It was only available to people who worked for the government.

Then in 1983, there was a terrible accident. A plane flew in the wrong place by mistake. It was not a government plane, so it did not have GPS. It flew over the private airspace of another country. That country's government shot the plane, and the plane crashed. Many people died. After the accident, the United States decided to let people outside of the government use GPS information. They wanted to prevent future accidents.

GPS measurements need two points: (1) a satellite in the sky and (2) a receiver on the ground. The radio waves go from the satellite to the receiver and back again. However, in order to get accurate information about a location on the ground, you need more than one satellite. You need four satellites.

The system is a little bit complicated, but here is how it works. The first measurement we need is distance. Let's say we want to know the location of a hospital. The radio waves can tell us how far the hospital is from the satellite. How? If you remember some math and science from your school days, you probably know the answer.

Distance = Rate x Time

- We know how fast radio waves travel. (= *Rate*)
- We can measure the time it takes for the waves to travel from the satellite to the hospital. (= *Time*)
- Simple math gives us the *Distance*.

But this is not enough to tell us the location of the building. We need to measure its distance from at least three different satellites. In the picture that follows, each circle is information from one satellite. The location of the hospital is where the three circles meet. A fourth satellite gives information about height of the location. (Perhaps the hospital is on a mountain.)

the hospital's location

When GPS first appeared, the technology was very expensive, and the receivers were quite large. But just like computers and phones, they got smaller and cheaper. Soon they were everywhere: inside cars, phones, and buildings. Today, there are more than a billion GPS receivers across the world.

What are all those receivers doing? Well, many of them are telling us where things are and how to find them. But GPS gives a lot of other information as well:

- Where is that coat I ordered online? When will it arrive?
- Is there a lot of traffic on the way to the city? Will it take 15 minutes or an hour to drive there?
- A ship in the middle of the Pacific Ocean is in trouble. How can we find it?
- How far do elephants walk to find food every day?

GPS can help us find the answers to these and many other questions.

Reflection

1. How do you think GPS can help answer the questions at the end of the reading?
2. You probably use GPS every day. How many uses can you name?

14

WINDSHIELD WIPERS

When we ride in the car or a bus on a rainy day, there they are, back and forth, back and forth. We look right past them, but they are working to keep us safe. Windshield wipers are one of those everyday objects that are a familiar part of our lives today. But cars did not start out with windshield wipers. Early cars did not have any glass in the front. In other words, they did not have a windshield (in the UK, it's called a *windscreen*), so of course, they had no wipers. It was not obvious that cars needed this new technology. Horses don't have wipers; why should cars have them?

Of course, that answer is obvious to us now: You need wipers to clean the windshield when it rains or snows. The idea for windshield wipers came to Mary Anderson on a wet and snowy day in 1902 when she was visiting New York. She was riding on a streetcar behind the driver. She could see that the driver was having trouble. Snow was falling on the windshield, and he could not see anything ahead of him. The windshield on this streetcar had several parts, and the driver could open one part and put his hand outside to clean off the snow. He did this every few minutes because the snow was very heavy. Every time he opened it, cold air and snow blew inside. All the passengers in the streetcar were cold, wet, and unhappy.

Anderson began to think of a solution to this problem. She started drawing a picture of her idea while she was on the streetcar. She designed a wiper made from rubber and wood. The wiper had a handle. When the driver pulled the handle, the wiper moved across the windshield. It cleaned off the snow and rain.

A great idea! Anderson probably made a lot of money for her invention, right? Wrong. Anderson did get a patent for her wipers in 1903. When an inventor gets a patent, it means that no one can steal his or her idea. A patent and its protection usually last for twenty years. But when Anderson tried to sell her idea to car companies, none of them was interested. Most of them did not think the invention was useful. Also, some of them believed that the wipers would be dangerous. They thought that the driver might watch the wipers instead of the road, and this might cause an accident. No one bought her invention.

Unfortunately, Anderson's idea came about ten or fifteen years too early. In 1903, there were streetcars, but not very many people owned cars. Henry Ford's first Model T did not appear until five years later. However, between 1908 and 1927, 15 million Model Ts rolled out of factories and onto American roads. And many of these cars had windshield wipers. Unfortunately, because patents only last for 20 years, Anderson's patent no longer protected her invention. That meant that car companies could use her idea, and they did not have to pay her. She never made any money.

Since then, there have been several improvements in windshield wipers. The most important one was the development of automatic wiper. The earlier wipers had to be turned on by the driver each time. At first, automatic wipers moved at just one speed. Then an inventor named Robert Kearns made an important improvement. His wipers allowed the driver to decide the speed of the wipers. Like Anderson, Kearns tried to sell his idea to car companies. And like Anderson, he had no success. Later he discovered that several car companies were using his ideas without paying for them. He was really angry! When Kearns died in 2005, he was still fighting with the car companies that stole his invention.

Windshield wipers on today's cars are based on ideas from both Anderson and Kearns. For example, all cars have wipers that move at different speeds. Modern wipers also include new ideas, like using a liquid to clean dirt and salt as well as rain and snow. Together they help to keep our cars running safely in all kinds of weather.

Reflection

1. Inventors like Anderson and Kearns face a lot of difficulties. What are some other challenges besides protecting their ideas?
2. Think of another invention that we look at or use every day but don't think about very much. When do you think it was invented? Do you know who invented it? How could you find out?

15

TRAFFIC LIGHTS

You may think traffic is bad now, but the traffic in London in the middle of the 19th century was really terrible. There were horses, bicycles, and streetcars everywhere. There were no traffic lights to control this traffic. It was a mess! And it was dangerous. More than a thousand people died in traffic accidents every year. Most of them were pedestrians; that is, people walking. On some of the busiest streets, policemen directed traffic. They used their hands to tell drivers and pedestrians when to move and when to stop. At night, it was even more dangerous. There was less traffic, but it was more difficult to see.

In 1866, an inventor offered a solution: the first traffic light. A policeman changed the light from red (for *stop*) to green (for *go*) and back again. These colors were used for trains, so it was natural to use them for traffic lights. Why red and green? The color red can be seen from the farthest distance. That makes it the best color to warn train drivers to stop.

At first, a white light was used for *go*, but this caused problems for two reasons. First, train drivers sometimes saw a bright star in the distance and thought it was the white light. Second, the red color of the light for *stop* comes from a piece of glass. The red glass covers a white light. If the red glass falls off (and sometimes it did), it leaves a white light. With a white light, the driver would continue instead of stopping. This was a dangerous possibility, so the railroads changed the color for *go* to green.

That first traffic light in London used gas, and it operated only at night. Unfortunately, after one month, there was an accident. The gas in the light exploded, and a police officer was badly injured. That was the end of traffic lights – for a while.

Soon, however, cars began to appear on the roads, and traffic got worse and worse. In New York City, it took 45 minutes to drive just 12 blocks. It was time for the traffic light to return.

There was not just one inventor of the modern traffic light. Several different inventors worked on the problem. As a result of their work, there were a number of different developments in the traffic light.

The first important improvement was the addition of a yellow light. The yellow light warned drivers that the light was going to change to red. With just two lights, drivers sometimes did not have enough time to stop. The yellow light reduced the number of accidents.

The increased use of electricity brought the next improvement: traffic lights became automatic. There was no need for a policeman to change the light every few minutes. Traffic engineers set each light to stay green or red for a certain amount of time. For how long? They just had to guess.

The purpose of these traffic lights was to manage traffic; in other words, all the cars. But starting in the 1930s, the lights began to include the needs of pedestrians. In cities where there were lots of pedestrians, WALK/DON'T WALK lights were added. Later, some lights began to warn pedestrians of the number of seconds left for the green light: 25, 24, 23.... Both of these developments made the streets safer for pedestrians.

In the 1960s, computers made it easier for engineers to make the time for each light different. Imagine: one street might have more traffic than another and need a longer green light. Or perhaps the traffic is heavier in the morning. New technology continued to improve traffic lights. Today, traffic lights are all connected in a system. Computers manage the system. In some cities, traffic lights can share information with cars. This information can help the system set the time for lights in the best possible way. The information can help cars move quickly and easily through the streets.

Traffic engineers believe that in the future, we may not need traffic lights anymore. Cars will have technology that lets them communicate with other cars. These cars will not have drivers. Computers inside the cars will control where they go and how fast they go. They will communicate with other cars and respond to conditions on the roads so that we all arrive safely. That day has not come yet, though, so pay attention to the traffic lights until then!

~

Reflection

1. How do you think traffic lights could be improved?
2. If you saw a red light in the middle of the night and there was no traffic on the other streets, would you go through the red light? Why or why not?

Made in the USA
Columbia, SC
02 June 2020